Insect World
Cockroaches
by Mari Schuh

Ideas for Parents and Teachers

Bullfrog Books let children practice reading informational text at the earliest reading levels. Repetition, familiar words, and photo labels support early readers.

Before Reading

- Discuss the cover photo. What does it tell them?

- Look at the picture glossary together. Read and discuss the words.

Read the Book

- "Walk" through the book and look at the photos. Let the child ask questions. Point out the photo labels.

- Read the book to the child, or have him or her read independently.

After Reading

- Prompt the child to think more. Ask: Have you ever seen a cockroach? Where was it? Was it eating anything?

Bullfrog Books are published by Jump!
5357 Penn Avenue South
Minneapolis, MN 55419
www.jumplibrary.com

Library of Congress Cataloging-in-Publication Data

Schuh, Mari C., 1975- author.
  Cockroaches / by Mari Schuh.
    pages cm. — (Insect world)
  Summary: "This photo-illustrated book for early readers tells how cockroaches find food and defend themselves from predators in the wild. Includes picture glossary" — Provided by publisher.
  Audience: Ages 5-8.
  Audience: K to grade 3.
  Includes index.
  ISBN 978-1-62031-161-5 (hardcover) —
  ISBN 978-1-62496-248-6 (ebook)
  1. Cockroaches — Juvenile literature. I. Title.
  QL505.5.S37 2015
  595.7'28 — dc23
                                    2014025459

Series Editor: Rebecca Glaser
Series Designer: Ellen Huber
Book Designer: Anna Peterson
Photo Researcher: Casie Cook

All photos by Shutterstock except: Alamy, 13; SuperStock, 16–17; Thinkstock, 10–11, 22.

Printed in the United States of America at Corporate Graphics in North Mankato, Minnesota.

Table of Contents

Night Bugs

Night is here.

A cockroach looks for food.

How will it find food?
Two antennas help
it smell.

Oh, wow!

They are long!

antenna

The cockroach eats
old plants.

Yum!

9

It eats dead bugs.

It eats rotting wood, too.

Chomp! Chomp!

Oh, no! A frog!

He is a predator.

He wants to eat the cockroach.

The bug lifts up its back end.
Hiss! Hiss! Go away!

The cockroach runs away.
It is fast. Look at it go.
Sharp claws help it run.

claw

14

It finds a pile
of wet leaves.

It hides there.

The pile is warm
and dark.

The cockroach rests.
Its flat body fits
in tiny spaces.

Later it will eat
more food.

Chomp! Chomp!

Parts of a Cockroach

antenna
A thin feeler that a cockroach uses to smell and feel.

spine
Sharp spines on its legs help a cockroach hold on tight.

head
A cockroach's head points down.

leg
A cockroach has six legs, like all insects.

Picture Glossary

claw
A hard, curved nail on a cockroach's foot.

predator
An animal that eats other animals for food.

dead
No longer living; a cockroach eats dead plants and animals.

rot
To break down and decay; rotting wood is soft and damp.

Index

To Learn More

Learning more is as easy as 1, 2, 3.

1) Go to www.factsurfer.com

2) Enter "cockroaches" into the search box.

3) Click the "Surf" button to see a list of websites.

With factsurfer.com, finding more information is just a click away.